AN ANALYSIS OF BENJAMIN N. CARDOZO'S THE NATURE OF THE JUDICIAL PROCESS

VOLUME 2, ISSUE 4 OF BRILLOPEDIA

ABHIRAMI THIRUMENI T AND AMALA I M

Contents

Preface

"Start writing, no matter what. The water does not flow until the faucet is turned on".

- Louis L'Amour

Hundreds of students and professors are contributing their work to Brillopedia, we are here to provide ample information about Law and Contemporary issues. Our aim is to provide a platform for today's generation to express their views and ideas on law and contemporary law.

Authors

Abhirami Thirumeni T

Amala I M

CHAPTER ONE

ABSTRACT

Benjamin Nathan Cardozo wrote the Nature of the Judicial Process in 1921. Cardozo was Associate Justice of the United States Supreme Court and Chief Justice of the New York Court of Appeals. Cardozo compiled the Nature of the Judicial Process from his lecture at Yale University. In this book Cardozo analyses and tries to answer how a judge decides a case. A judge uses various methods like philosophy, history, custom, justice and morals and social welfare. In the end, whichever method the judge uses, it must be in conformity with social welfare as it is the final cause. There are four lectures in this book. The first lecture deals with introduction and the method of philosophy. The second lecture deals with the methods of history, tradition and sociology. The third lecture deals with the method of sociology and the judge as a legislator. The final lecture deals with adherence to precedent, the subconscious element of judicial process and conclusion. Each of these lectures is intended to be discussed in this paper.

CHAPTER TWO

INTRODUCTION

Cardozo begins by asking a series of questions to himself regarding how a case is being decided in the courts. In the decision-making process, the Judge uses various ingredients like logical consistency, custom, precedent, social welfare, morals and justice into the strange compound brewed daily in the caldron of the courts. Cardozo considered the Judge made laws one of life's existing realities. According to him, the law involves some governing principles. However, not the same principles are followed by all jurists or even a uniform principle for any one judge in every case. The principle may sometimes be consciously chosen or subconsciously derived, yet inherently personal.[1]

Cardozo points out that the first inquiry should be on the question: where does the Judge find the law he embodies in his judgement? He answers that there are times when the source is quite obvious. It might be the Constitution or the statute. The Judge has to look no further if the law is given in the Constitution or the statute.[2] It is to be noted that the Constitution overrides the statute, and if the statute is in consistent with the Constitution, it overrides the judge-made laws. Hence, judge-made laws of secondary and subordinate to the laws made by the Legislature.

Even if the law is given in the code or statute, the work of a judge cannot be said to be mechanical. There may arise gaps to be filled, ambiguities to be cleared, and wrongs to be mitigated if not avoided. Interpretation means understanding the Legislature's mind.[3] The difficulties of interpretation arise when the Legislature has no meaning at all. When the Legislature did not discuss the question which came before the Judge at the time of making the legislation, the Judge should guess what would be in the minds of the Legislature if the question came before the Legislature.

As an interpreter of the community, the Judge must supply omissions, correct uncertainty and harmonise results with justice through a method of free decision - *LibreRechercheScientifique.*[4]

When the Constitution and statute are silent, the Judge must look into the common law to find thc rule that fits the case. The first thing the Judge has to do is compare the case before him with the precedents. When the precedent is exactly similar to the case before him, he can apply it just like a statute. A judge may match the colour of the case at hand against the colours of many sample cases spread out on his desk.[5] The sample nearest in the shade will apply the applicable rule. But in such a case, no new law will evolve. The man with the best card index of cases will be considered the wisest Judge. When the colours do not match, when the reference in the index fails, when there is no decisive precedent, the real work of the Judge begins. He must then fashion law for the case before him. Every judgment has a generative power. There is a human tendency to reproduce of a similar kind. The sentence of today will make the right and wrong of tomorrow.[6] A sentence may be pronounced based on one of the many principles in law. Once a judgment is being pronounced, it becomes a new stock of descent. It becomes a source from which new principles or norms may arise. Not all progeny of principles in a judgment survives. Those that cannot prove their worth and strength by the test of experience are considered void.

The rules and principles of case laws are never treated as final truths. They are considered as working hypotheses which are continuously retested in the great laboratories of the law, that is, the courts of justice. If a rule continually brings out injustice, it is reformulated. The process of this reformulation or the work of modification is gradual. It goes on inch by inch. Its effects are measured by decades and even centuries. What was once thought to be an exception is the rule of today and what was the rule is now the exception.[7]

The problem which confronts a judge is a twofold one. He must first extract from the precedents the underlying principle, that is, the *ratio decidendi*, and secondly, he must then determine the path or direction along which the principle is to move and develop; if it is not, it will wither and die.[8]

To extract the underlying principle from the precedent is not very easy. The obiter dictum must be stripped off and cast aside. It is difficult to separate the accidental and nonessential from the essential and inherent.[9]

Once the underlying principle is separated from the precedent, the path or direction along which the principle should move and develop should be determined. For this, Cardozo suggested the following four methods that judges used:

1. Logical progression - The rule of analogy or the method of philosophy
2. Historical development - The method of evolution
3. The customs of the community - The method of tradition
4. Justice, morals and social welfare - The method of sociology

[1]__BENJAMIN N CARDOZO, THE NATURE OF THE JUDICIAL PROCESS 10 (Oxford University Press 1946).
[2]__*Id.* at 14.
[3]__*Id.* at 15.
[4]__*Id.* at 16.
[5]__*Id.* at 21.
[6]__*Id.*
[7]__*Id.* at 23.
[8]__*Id.* at 28.
[9]__*Id.* at 29.

CHAPTER THREE

THE METHOD OF PHILOSOPHY

Cardozo considers the method of philosophy to be first among the other principles used to select the path on which a principle should develop. He thinks of the method of philosophy first not because it is the most important but because it comes from natural, orderly, and logical succession. He also points out that some great judges have considered the method of philosophy to mean little or nothing in law. In the case *Quinn v. Leathem,*[1] LordHalsbury has said that logical reasoning assumes that law is necessarily a logical code, whereas law is not always logical. Cardozo defends the statement of Holmes, "the life of the law has not been logic; it has been experience"[2] by stating that Holmes has not said that logic is not to be considered when experience is silent.

Cardozo says that the symmetry of legal structure should not be disturbed by introducing inconsistencies, irrelevancies and artificial exceptions unless there is some sufficient reason which may be history, custom, policy or justice. If there is no such reason, a Judge must be logical, just like how a Judge should be impartial. While deciding on similar cases, the parties expect the same decision. If a case was decided against a person yesterday when he was the defendant, he would expect the decision in favour of him for the same set of facts if today he is the plaintiff. It would be a gross injustice to decide cases on the same points on opposite principles. Hence, the same question cannot be decided in one way for one set of litigants and in another way for another set of litigants. Therefore, if the litigants should have faith in the even-handed administration of justice in the courts, adherence to precedents must be the rule.

Sometimes, two or more principles followed with logic can be applied to a case. One principle or precedent with a logic may point to one conclusion, and another principle or precedent followed by a logic will point to another conclusion. In such cases, the Judge must decide between the two paths, and such a decision will be choosing one of the two principles or deriving a third principle which may be a combination of the first two principles. To explain this, Cardozo illustrates the case, *Riggs v. Palmer*.[3] There were three principles upon which the case could be decided, and the Court had to choose one. The first principle was that the will has a binding force disposing of the testator's estate in conformity with the law. This principle, pushed to the limit of its logic, upholds the title of the murderer. The second principle is that the civil courts may not add to the pains and penalties of crimes. This principle, pushed to the limit of its logic, also upholds the title of the murderer. The third principle is that no man should take advantage of his own wrong. The logic of this principle prevailed over the logic of the other principles. The murderer lost the legacy for which he murdered because the social interest was served by refusing the criminal to profit from his crime. It was greater than the preservation and enforcement of legal rights of ownership. Different analogies, precedents and principles can be applied to a case, but the most fundamental principle that represents the larger and deeper social interest is chosen.

Judges follow logic, analogies and philosophies till they reach a certain point. At first, the paths will be clear, and they will follow the same lines. But at a certain point, the path will begin to diverge, and the Judge has to choose between the diverged paths. At this point, history, custom, social welfare or justice comes to rescue the anxious Judge and tells him where to go.

The fundamental concepts given in a decision will be equivocal in the beginning. New cases extract its essence and new rules and principles emerge and become a datum. From the point of departure new lines will run. When the principle formulated is too narrow or too broad, it has to be reformulated. The rules and principles change such that its origins get forgotten and it becomes a new stock of descent.[4]

Cardozo uses the word philosophy to include syllogism to analogy. All these words have a nexus to logic. They are inspired by the same principles of consistency, certainty and uniformity of plan and structure. All these are intended towards unity where differences will be reconciled and abnormalities will vanish.

Cardozo considers that the misuse of logical method begins when the method is treated as final and supreme.

[1] [1901] UKHL 2.

[2] THE COMMON LAW, O. W. HOLMES, JR. Boston 1 (Little, Brown and Company, 1881).

[3] 115 N.Y. 506 (1889).

[4] BENJAMIN N CARDOZO, THE NATURE OF THE JUDICIAL PROCESS 48 (Oxford University Press 1946).

CHAPTER FOUR

THE METHODS OF HISTORY, TRADITION AND SOCIOLOGY

History enables us to make the path of logic clear.[1] The path of logic can be made clear by history when the logic is in consistency with the past or in consistency with some pre-established norm. Some concepts in law owe their existing form almost exclusively to history. They are to be understood only as historical growths. In the development of such principles, history is likely to predominate over logic.[2] In other concepts, even though they have history which shapes them, logic is likely to predominate over history. History illuminates the past, and in so doing could guide the future path of the law. We study the past events so that it does not paralyse today and today does not paralyse tomorrow.[3] Sometimes conceptions of law are unintelligible or arbitrary when they are separated from their past form and meaning. In order for these to be logical, one must consider their origins.

The words of Maitland are borrowed by Cardozo to sharpen the importance of this method. Giving 'Law of Property' as the readiest example, Cardozo clarifies that there are certain fields where there can be no progress without history. Philosophy also plays its role here. Borrowing the examples and theories of Maitland, Holmes and Pound, Cardozo envisages a couple of areas history fostered and must tend to shape.

Cardozo has used concepts from land law and contract law to illustrate the growth which history has fostered and which history must tend to shape. There are times when the subject matter does not clearly show which method is used, in such cases the judge determines the choice of paths. Cardozo uses an illustration given by Pound to explain this. The illustration which Cardozo takes is whether the gift of movable property between living persons is effective without delivery. To decide cases in this issue, some judges have used analogy of the Roman law, others have used the history of forms of conveyance, and some have used the analysis of fundamental concepts and the results of such analysis to logical conclusions. They are often times when the two methods supplement each other. Which method will predominate in the case may depend.[4]

If philosophy and history do not serve to fix the direction of a principle, custom may step into the picture. Cardozo rejects Coke's theory that the common law is separated from customs. Cardozo quotes Blackstone that the common law is properly distinguishable into three kinds:

1. *General customs* : These are the universal rule for the whole of England and form the common law.
2. *Particular Customs* : These are for the inhabitants of particular districts.
3. *Certain particular laws* : These are by custom adopted and used by some particular courts of pretty general and extensive jurisdiction.

Undoubtedly, the usage of custom in the development of common law is comparatively less today than it was in the earlier times. In the words of pound, today we recognize that the custom is a custom of judicial decision, not of popular action. In the words of Gray, it is doubtful whether throughout the legal history, the rules laid down by the judges have not generated custom rather than the custom generated the rules. Today we look at a custom not for the creation of new rules but for tests and standards to determine how established rules shall be applied. When customs intend to create a new law there is a tendency in the courts to leave such developments to the legislation. When custom is to be applied, we must determine whether there has been adherence or departure.

It must be noted that each method maintains an interaction between life and the law (or conduct and order). Life casts the moulds of conduct which will someday become fixed as law. Law preserves the moulds, which have taken form and shape from life.[5]

When the question arises as to what we are supposed to be consistent with: philosophy, history or custom, the answer is that when some legal concepts have shown largely historical growth, history will be guiding the path; when certain large and fundamental concepts whose comparative jurisprudence shows to be common, the larger scope shall be given to logic and symmetry; when some rules are with approximately the same convenience which are to be settled one way or the other, custom tends to assert itself as the controlling force in guiding the choice of paths.[6] When the social needs demand for a settlement rather than the other, in such cases we must bend symmetry, ignore history and sacrifice custom in the pursuit of other and larger ends. With this, the power of social justice finds its way by the method of sociology.

Cardozo points out that the final cause of law is the welfare of society.[7] Accordingly, logic, history and custom have their place in shaping law but only within bound. The end which the law serves, *i.e.,* social welfare will dominate logic, history and custom. Hence, when judges are to decide the limits of existing rules (to how far it should be extended or restricted) they must let the welfare of society fix the path.[8] Judges cannot make or remove rules at their pleasure in accordance with the changing views of expediency or wisdom.[9] Like we had earlier seen in Lecture 1, courts apply rules which are derived from legal principles and judicial precedents and in order to obtain uniformity, consistency and certainty we must apply these rules unless it is unreasonable. But this doesn't mean that there are no gaps. In the words of Holmes, "I recognise without hesitation that judges must and do legislate, but they do so only interstitially; they are confined from molar to molecular motions. A common law judge could not say, I think the doctrine of consideration is a bit of historical nonsense and shall not enforce it in my court."

When the statute does not go into the details and particulars, but just contains the general principles, the legislation has less tendency to limit the freedom of the judge while interpreting to fill the gaps. This is why there is greater freedom of choice in the construction of constitution (as constitutions are more likely to enunciate general principles) than that of ordinary statutes. But the real concern is not the size of the gaps rather it is the principle that determines how the gap is to be filled. The method of sociology in the filling of gaps puts its emphasis on social welfare.[10] Cardozo uses the word sociology to mean public policy, or adherence to the standards of right conduct, which find expression in the mores of the community. Hence, it is based on religion, ethics, social sense of justice, etc.

Cardozo points out that recently, the social value of a rule has become a test of growing power and importance in every branch of law. This is shown in the words of Dean Pound "Perhaps the most significant advance in the modern science of law is the change from the analytical to the functional attitude."

In some departments of law, the method of sociology is in harmony with the method of philosophy or of evolution or of tradition. In such fields, logic, coherence and consistency are still sought as ends. Hence, in such areas, we pursue logic and coherence and consistency as the greater social values.

Cardozo says that there are a few broad areas where the method of sociology has fruitful application. The first of these areas is the constitution, then the branches of private law when public policy has its importance and finally other areas where this method is less insistent and pervasive.

When Cardozo first analyses the constitution, he begins with the provision that No one shall be deprived of liberty without due process of law. Here the term liberty is not defined. Liberty was considered at first static and absolute. It was so enshrined in the Declaration of Independence, the blood of Revolution was also based on this, the political philosophy of Rousseau, Locke, Herbert Spencer and of the Manchester School of Economists had dignified and rationalised it. But today we know that the term liberty does not have a static meaning in every generation, what was arbitrary once is lawful today and what is arbitrary today may become lawful tomorrow. The idea of the 19th century was that the exact rule of every case should be reached by an absolute process of logical deduction and it was considered to be the very idea of justice. Dicey in his book Law and Opinion in England quotes that "The movement from individualistic liberalism (liberty of individuals was considered most important) to unsystematic collectivism (the social welfare and liberty was considered important. This change from individual to society, limited the liberty of individuals)" had brought changes in the social order which carried with them the need of a new formulation of fundamental rights and duties. Hence, gradually, the significance of constitutional limitations in the domain of individual liberty gained recognition and dominance. In the case *Hurtado v. California,*[11] Judge Hough quotes that if the new epoch had then dawned, it was still obscured by fog and cloud. This means that even if the new period had started, it is still concealed and vague with fog and cloud. Scattered rays of light may have signalled the coming day. But they were not enough to blaze the path.[12]

When courts decide on statutes, the decisions should not be based on the abstract principles or the guidance of an ideal community, rather it should be based on the present day conditions. An example, where a statute forbidding night work for women was declared to be arbitrary in 1907 was in 1915 considered to be valid and reasonable.

Cardozo also uses the phrase equal protection of laws to explain how the constitution is to be interpreted using sociology. In a narrow sense this phase may seem to foster inequality but in a broad sense we can understand that it is to establish equality of position between parties. Hence, it can be concluded that constitutional immunities are not constant and it varies from time to time. Statutes are made to meet the current needs. When the needs change, amendments are required. But a constitution gives rules for the passing hour but for an expanding future. Interpretations to the constitution give details and particulars and thereby it loses its flexibility and its meaning gets hardened. But it maintains its power of adaptation. Even in the interpretation of statutes, the meaning of today is not the meaning of tomorrow.

We may use the same principles and rules but with different meanings. We do not inquire what the legislature meant years ago but we would have inquired what would have been its meaning if they had known our present conditions. Hence, the interpretation of statute must never remain the same forever. Hence, if the meaning of a statue is the same from the beginning to the end of its day, then such a meaning is erroneous. New times and new manners may call for new standards and new rules.[13]

Therefore, the judges are free to mark the limits of individual freedom and shape their judgements in accordance with justice and reason. But this doesn't mean that the judges while interpreting statutes can substitute their idea of reason and justice instead of those men and women who deserve the justice. So the judge has to see what a man of normal intellect and conscience may reasonably look upon as right. Hence, an interpreter must put aside his political and legislative values and interpret objectively according to the social life of the community whose interests are to be protected. There are times when the judge can act subjectively. These are the times when the judge has to decide the statutes are arbitrary and oppressive. When the court exercises the right of supervision, there is no danger of abuse.

In the view of the critics of this existing system, when the legislature makes a statute that creates hardship to individuals or classes and is absurd, we must trust legislatures for undoing the wrong. But Cardozo believes that there must be an external restraining power of the judiciary over the legislative judgment so that by conscious or subconscious influence of the presence of this restraining power in the background the legislature tends to stabilise and rationalise its legislative judgment and try to avoid or remove such errors. There are also times when the legislature has disregarded their own responsibility of correcting the errors and have passed it to the courts for judicial review. Hence there shouldn't be a complete independence from restraint to the public officers elected.[14]

This restraining power of the judiciary is not only exercised in a few cases where the legislature has gone beyond the lines that marked the limits of discretion. Its chief worth can be found in making vocal and audible the ideals that might otherwise be silenced. This power should be exercised by the judiciary with insight into social values.[15]

Another field where the method of sociology has a dominance is in the case of the rules in private law. There are some rules of private law which have been shaped in the creation by public policy. When judges are deciding a case regarding the rule of policy which was in existence 100 or 150 years ago, the judges should consider what the rule of policy should be for the present time. Hence if the originally well founded rules are arbitrary in the current circumstances, it needs to be changed according to the existing conditions.[16]

[1] *Id.* at 51.

[2] *Id.* at 52.

[3] *Id.* at 54.

[4] *Id.* at 58.

[5] *Id.* at 64.

[6] *Id.* at 65.

[7] *Id.* at 66.

[8] *Id.* at 67.

[9] *Id.* at 68.

[10] *Id.* at 71.

[11] 110 U.S. 516 (1884).

[12] *Id.* at 79.

[13] *Id.* at 88.

[14] *Id.* at 90.

[15] *Id.* at 94.

[16] *Id.* at 96.

CHAPTER FIVE

THE METHOD OF SOCIOLOGY. THE JUDGE AS A LEGISLATOR

Cardozo begins this lecture by stating that there is no branch of law where the method of sociology is not fruitful.[1] Even in branches of law where the method is not dominant, it is always present in some minimal form. It acts as an arbiter between other methods and allows to balance and harmonise between the methods.

The rules may have its old form but when time passes, they are filled with new content. The end which the law serves is the task of service and for this the rules must be altered if it is out of date. This concept of end of the law to determine the direction of growth of law was a contribution of Jhering which was based on the method of sociology.[2] The choice of path must depend on knowing what it will lead us to.

We do not pick our rules of the law fully blossomed from the trees.[3] These are made by judges with the passage of time. When the judges shape the law, they must heed to the mores of that present time. Law has a historical growth. It is an expression of the customary morality which has developed from one age to another.The judge and also the legislator has to apply his mind to attain the moral end and this embodiment in the legal forms. This can be done only with adequate conscious effort to understand the life of the community. It is the duty of the judge to declare the law in accordance with reason and Justice as well as in accordance with custom. It is the customary morality of the right minded men and women which he is to enforce by his decree. Hence when the court decides the case, he must look on to the notions of rights and wrong prevalent in the community, the mores of the time.[4] Usually when the judge decides the case is guided by his own notions of right and wrong which are prevalent in his community. When the judge has to decide between his individual (subjective) view or that of the general conscience (objective) he has to go objectively.[5]

Cardozo says that analysis of the judicial process is that logic, history, custom and utility are the accepted standards of right conduct.[6] This may be applied as a single or in combination to shape the progress of the law.Which one of these will dominate will depend upon the value of the social interests that will be affected. One of the most important social interests is that the law should be uniform and impartial. There should be no action which is even arbitrary. There shall be systematic development, consistency with history, or custom when custom has been the motive force. But systematic development may be bought at too high a price.[7] Uniformity ceases to be a good when it becomes uniformity of oppression. The social interest served by the symmetry of sovereignty must then be balanced against the social interest served by equity and fairness or other elements of social welfare. At this point the judge takes the path along new courses making a point of departure. The judge knows which social interest outweighs the author by his experience, study and reflection. Here we can see that there is a point of contact between the legislator's work and the judge's work. Each is legislating within their limits of competence. The limit of the judge is narrower than that of the legislator as he legislates only to fill the gaps in the law. Hence, the law is being made and not found.[8]

Even a slight change in the habits of the public leads to a reconsideration of the law. The process of research done by the judge is very analogous (similar) to that of a legislator. A situation arises and the law needs to adapt to that situation and it must be according to justice and social utility. The distinction is that the legislator is not hampered by any limitations in the appreciation of a general situation whereas a judge when he addresses a case, the problem is concrete and he must adhere to it and avoid dangers of arbitrary action.[9] The base of his judicial decision should be on the elements of an objective nature.[10]

The theory of the older writers was that judges did not legislate at all. A pre-existing rule was there which was concealed in the body of the customary law. All that the judges did was to throw off the wrappings and expose the statute to our view. According to Gray, it is believed that customs are not law even though it is firmly established until it is adopted by the courts. Even statutes are not laws because the court has to fix their meaning.[11] Law is what judges declare and statutes, precedents, opinions of experts, customs and morality are sources of law.

Statutes do not cease to be law because the power to fix their meaning in case of doubt or ambiguity is with the Courts. There arises times when the court has to overrule its own decisions. Even the courts may have to overrule retrospectively. But these are rare circumstances and hence need not worry about diverse judgment.

Judges have the power to go beyond the bounds set by precedents and custom. But if judges do this with a guilty and evil mind, they will be removed even though the judgment may stand. The law of nature is no longer conceived as static and eternal. It does not override positive law. It is from which the positive law is woven. The growth of the law of nature is a long and interesting chapter in jurisprudence. The doctrine reached its highest development with the Stoics which profoundly influenced the ideals of men in statecraft and in law. Later the rise and dominance of analytical school led to the abandonment of natural law. Thereafter, there was a revival of natural law in an altered form. The old theory survived a little more than the name.

It is the duty of the judge to maintain a relation between law and morals, reason and good conscience within his limited power of innovation. The function of our courts is to keep the doctrines up to date with the mores by restatement and giving them new content. This is judicial legislation and the judge legislates at his peril. When this duty of legislation is entrusted with the judiciary, a brave and honest judge does not fear the perils.

There can be no assurance given that the judges will interpret the mores wisely and truly than any other man. But, the power of interpretation is entrusted upon them by the constitution and they are to fulfil their functions as judges by acting with conscience and intelligence to attain their conclusions a fair advantage of truth and wisdom. Their conclusions are subject to constant testing and retesting, revision and readjustment.

All that the method of sociology demands is that within the narrow range of choice, the judge has to search for social justice and decide accordingly.[12]

In France, there was a revolt against the existing order of jurisprudence during 1904. Every case they decided was by considering how a good man may do and render judgment accordingly. This was done when there was inconsistency in statutes.[13]

When the statute and precedent does not provide the law, the judge has to assume the role of the legislator. Even when we say a judge is free, he is not free to decide at his pleasure or at his own idea of good. He has to exercise this discretion informed by tradition, methodised by analogy, disciplined by system and subordinated to social welfare.[14]

[1] *Id.* at 98.
[2] *Id.* at 102.
[3] *Id.* at 103.
[4] *Id.* at 104.
[5] *Id.* at 106.
[6] *Id.* at 112.
[7] *Id.* at 112.
[8] *Id.* at 115.
[9] *Id.* at 120.
[10] *Id.* at 121.
[11] *Id.* at 125.
[12] *Id.* at 137.
[13] *Id.* at 139.
[14] *Id.* at 141.

CHAPTER SIX

ADHERENCE TO PRECEDENT

In a vast majority of cases, the retrospective effect in judge-made laws have either no hardship or only such hardship which is inevitable where there is no rule.[1] When the hardship is more then the retrospective operation is withheld. When a final court of appeal decides a statute as void and later reverses its own judgment and declares the statute valid, between the time period of declaring void and then valid, there are transactions being carried out and its validity will be a question. Most of the Court by relying on the principle of realism have held that the operation of the statute has been suspended in such an interval.[2] When we decide such cases, it shall be done by considering the sentiments of justice and not by metaphysical conceptions of the nature of judge-made laws.[3]

Cardozo says that adherence to precedent should be the rule and not the exception.[4] The workload of the judges will increase to a breaking point if they are to reopen every decided case if there is no adherence to precedent. A case decided in one way might turn in another way if heard again by another bench and this goes on. Hence, in such circumstances, there is nothing to be done rather than to stand by the errors that were decided at the first time. Cardozo also points out that the rule of adherence to precedent should be relaxed to some extent. When a rule was tested by experience and was found to be inconsistent with justice or social welfare, there should not be any hesitation to reformulate it or to abandon it.

If the judges have misinterpreted the mores of their day, or if the mores of their day are not suitable for the present day, then it should be allowed to be changed by the successors.

The judge must balance all the ingredients, ie, philosophy, logic, analogies, history, custom, sense of right, and adding a little here and taking out a little there. He must determine as wisely as he can. A judge has to distinguish between the precedents which are merely static and those which are dynamic. A majority of cases have a semblance of reason that can be decided only in one way. There is a percentage of cases which is neither too small nor too large, where the decision will affect the future and the development of law.[5] These are the cases where the creative element in the judicial process finds its opportunity and power.

There may be one or more conclusions that can be applied in a case. In such circumstances, there requires balancing of judgment, testing and sorting of considerations of analogy and logic and utility and fairness. Here it is that the judge assumes the function of a lawgiver. Cardozo thereafter explained his personal experience in the judicial process.

[1] *Id.* at 147.

[2] Harris v. Jex, 55 N. Y. 421.

[3] *Id.* at 148.

[4] *Id.* at 149.

[5] *Id.* at 165.

CHAPTER SEVEN

THE SUBCONSCIOUS ELEMENT IN THE JUDICIAL PROCESS

Earlier, we had seen that there are many forces that the judge uses to shape their judgments. These forces are not chosen in many cases by consciousness. Deep below the consciousness there are other forces, the likes and dislikes, the predilections and prejudices, the complex of instincts and emotions and habits and convictions, which make the man, whether he be litigant or judge. Judges are also subject to human limitations.

Judicial power is never exercised for the purpose of giving effect to the will of the judge, it is always used for the purpose of giving effect to the will of the legislature; in other words, to the will of the law. The legal principle which is to be applied in a case appears as an initial cause, from which one has drawn the result which is found deduced from it.[1]

The duty of a judge is to objectify in law, and not the aspirations and convictions and philosophies of the judge himself, but the aspirations and convictions and philosophies of the men and women of that time. A judge will not be able to do his duty wll, if his sympathies, beliefs and passionate devotions are with a time that is in the past.

A person will not be made a judge, unless such person has absorbed the spirit, and has filled themselves with a love for the law and the people. Hence, judges must have sympathy with the spirit of their times.

The training of the judge with judicial temperament, will help in some degree to emancipate him from the suggestive power of individual dislikes and prepossessions. It will help to broaden the group to which his subconscious loyalties are due. Never will these loyalties be utterly extinguished while human nature is what it is. [2]

The eccentricities of judges balance one another. One judge looks at problems from the point of view of history, another from the point of philosophy, another from that of social utility. The flaws are there as in every human institution. We have faith that they will be corrected. There is no assurance that the rule of the majority will be the expression of perfect reason when embodied in constitution or in statute. [3]

[1] *Id.* at 170.
[2] *Id.* at 176.
[3] *Id.* at 177.

CHAPTER EIGHT

CONCLUSION

Cardozo concludes by stating that the work of a judge is, in one sense, to be enduring and, in another sense, ephemeral. What is good in it endures. What is erroneous is pretty sure to perish. The good remains the foundation on which new structures will be built. The bad will be rejected and cast off in the laboratory for years. Little by little, the old doctrine is not to be found. Often the encroachments are so gradual that their significance is at first not visible. Finally, we discover that the entire principle has been changed and gives rise to new ones.[1]

In the making of law, there are chances for errors. A judge must not worry too much about such errors. It is humane to have errors. They may render a little confusion for a time. In the end, such errors will be modified or corrected. In the endless process of testing and retesting, there is constant rejection of the rules and principles and constant retention of whatever is pure, sound, and fine.[2]

[1] *Id.* at 178.

[2] *Id.* at 179.